Exurbia

Books by Andy Brown

Poetry
The Fool and the Physician (Salt, 2012)
Goose Music (Salt, 2008, with John Burnside)
Fall of the Rebel Angels: Poems 1996-2006 (Salt, 2006)
Hunting the Kinnayas (Stride, 2004)
From a Cliff (Arc, 2002)
The Wanderer's Prayer (Arc, 1999)
West of Yesterday (Stride, 1998)

Poetry Chapbooks
The Storm Berm (tall-lighthouse, 2008)
The Trust Territory (Heaventree, 2005)
Of Science (Worple Press, 2001, with David Morley)
Sleight of Foot (Reality Street 4 Packs, 1998)
The Sleep Switch (Odyssey, 1996)

Editor
The Writing Occurs As Song: A Kelvin Corcoran Reader (Shearsman 2014)
The Allotment: new lyric poets (Stride, 2006)
Binary Myths 1 & 2: correspondences with poets and poet-editors (Stride, 2004)

EXURBIA

Andy Brown

First published in 2014 by
Worple Press
Achill Sound, 2b Dry Hill Road
Tonbridge
Kent TN9 1LX.
www.worplepress.co.uk

© Copyright Andy Brown

The moral right of the author has been asserted in accordance with the Copyrights, Designs and Patents Act of 1988. All rights reserved.

Cover image by Corinna Wagner

No part of this work covered by the copyright thereon may be reproduced or used in any means – graphic, electronic, or mechanical, including copying, recording, taping, or information storage or retrieval systems – without written permission of the publisher.

Printed by imprintdigital
Upton Pyne, Exeter
www.imprintdigital.net

Typeset by narrator
www.narrator.me.uk
info@narrator.me.uk

ISBN: 978-1-905208-24-1

Acknowledgements

Grateful thanks to the editors of the following journals, anthologies and chapbooks where these poems, or versions of them, were originally published:
Acumen, Agenda, The Camarillo Review, City Lighthouse, Earthlines, Entanglements: new ecopoetry, The Flying Post, Identity Parade, Life Writing, The Long Poem Magazine, Other Voices International, Peninsula, Poetry Review, Proof, Shearsman, The Storm Berm, This Line Is Not For Turning, UPLIFT: A Samizdat for Lee Harwood, A View From the Lighthouse, Wild Devon, Writers' Forum, 'Wall of Miracles' Installation Exeter University.

Special thanks to Verle Swenters at the Shoes or No Shoes Museum, Belgium, for commissioning 'Lost Shoes' for the museum's collection (www.shoesornoshoes.com), and to Corinna Wagner – enthusiast, collaborator, sharer of ideas and days.

Contents

1

Lost Shoes	3
Caliology	5
Hamlin Lane	6
The Last Thatch	7
Foreign News	8
Things	9
Becoming	11
Happiness	12
A Lover's Discourse	13
Self Portrait at the Year's Turning	15
Blackbird	16
Suburban Plot	17
Cemetery Song	19
'The Rain Falls Gently on the Town'	20
After Bottling	21
Picking Bullaces	23
Rewriting the Ground	24
Selvage	25
Home / Leaving	28

2

The Outskirts	33

3

Homing	41
Lambing at Gwernllertai	42
The Woolbrook	43
Pen y Fan	44
How to Pay Attention	45
The Wood for the Trees	46
Crow Wedding	47

On Coupling	49
Two Birdstrikes	50
Nocturne	51
Forest	52
Learning the Names	54
Harbour Blues	55
The Storm Berm	56
A Beach	57
Seascape with Kites and Gulls	58
Song of the Lifeboat Men's Daughters	59
A Ship in a Bottle	60
Along the Tide Wash	62
It Happens When You Look Away	64
Matriline	65
Planktos	66
The Last Geese	67

1

*'People wish to be settled;
only as far as they are unsettled
is there any hope for them.'*

Ralph Waldo Emerson

Lost Shoes

Abandoned footwear – Dress Shoes and Sneakers –
litters forsaken locations. By busy roadsides
and distant reservoirs, Slip-Ons and High Heels
converge on the verges. On riverbanks,

along the margins of lonely ponds, fishermen
haul-up rank Gumboots and Deck Shoes, missing
Brogues, a puzzling Stiletto or Kitten Heel, as though
they've stumbled on an ill-dressed scene, a crime.

And sleeping there above the flotsam line
amongst the husks of fish and tangled nets,
the bladder wrack and ocean's castoffs,
a lover may notice a Flip Flop or Mule,

or stumble across the rarer find of a single
Sling-Back or Jazz Shoe, dropped over the bows
of some expensive yacht as it slooped its way
across the waves in New Year's reveries.

Or yet still on building sites, in car parks
and subways, a solitary Oxford or an Espadrille
lingers in the grime and debris, calling to its other.
And who has not passed through a summer field

to find, decaying in the corn, a Sandal or a Ballet Flat,
a Moccasin, or Work Boot that some farmer,
startled by the presence of the overlooked
scarecrow, lost in his retreat through the stubble;

or the scarecrow himself, loping away from
his hitch-post at midnight, who kicked a leg
and shucked a Runner, a Track Spike, a Clog
forever abandoned to yield a home to mice?

There's a Glass Slipper on every palace driveway.
New shoes, old shoes, leather shoes that linger
for forty years beneath suburban bushes. A Blücher
in a park hut. That Snow Shoe jutting from a bin…

Ten thousand shoes misplaced or chucked on purpose,
tossed by their laces to hang from the branches of trees,
to dangle over power lines at crossroads.
Your empty Wellington Boots, lolling in the hall.

Caliology

the study of birds' nests

Magpie nest displayed in the Hunterian Museum,
Glasgow, natural materials and found metal.

A magpie's dream of twisted sticks and steel –
this bowl of twigs, barbed-wire and coat hangers
designed for hanging shirts, or barring thieves,
now stuck with mud and gardeners' skewers
and turned to the purpose of cradling eggs.
Perhaps it was the metal's tempting glint,
or something of its 'inner architect'
that made the bird suppose these things might bend
beneath the pressure of a well-placed bill;
that these collected charms might just become
girders strong enough to shore up brushwood
and fragile stalks of grass against their ruin.
How shall we build our homes? Of what? And where?
Here comes the magpie's answer, on the air.

Hamlin Lane

This New Year's Day we've come to get away
from ourselves, digging land put by for common use;
weeding-out the pale rhizomes of couch grass,
those unrelenting roots that choke our beds.

This morning there is nothing more real
than *here* where boot meets shovel, shovel earth;
the earth's throat singing worms for hungry birds.

Across the Rec., where the broad estate hunkers,
bonfires climb the ladders of their smoke. The plot
beneath our boots reads like a page of invisible ink;

a book that writes itself when April wakes the seeds
and the dreaming dormice in the compost heap.
Above us, airplane contrails criss-cross space –
that longing all things share: to last *and* fade.

The Last Thatch

for Thomas Lynch

The sun had dried the haggard to a crust,
whilst up on Riley's roof they hammered slates.
The donkey's hooves were puffing up the dust

as we listened to the roofers' repartee – they cussed
each time their new apprentice made mistakes.
The sun had dried the haggard to a crust.

*'You need to watch your bloody work. A hefty gust
might see you boost the unemployment rates…'*
The donkey's hooves were puffing up the dust

below, tired of the heat and apparently nonplussed
that soon he'd face the derby's starting gates.
The sun had dried the haggard to a crust.

Racing themselves, the roofers said they must
'*Get the whole shebang finished before eight*',
when donkey hooves would puff the racetrack dust.

The thatch was gone; the new slates 'more robust';
the starter's gun discharged on real estate.
The sun had dried the racetrack to a crust
where donkey hooves were puffing up the dust.

Foreign News

An Englishman abroad in borrowed shoes
upsets his coffee cup at breaking news:
four explosions back at home in London.

A foreign coolness steals around his neck,
as when the impossible rubs shoulders
with what we understand as being real.

Across the flood of global reportage,
the thrum of local traffic: buses, cars,
the island ferryboat's horn; everyone
going about the business of their day,

as his son stumbles into the kitchen
his hands held-out and warmly cupped around
the body of a wounded garden thrush
the neighbour's wilful cat has just delivered.

Things

Not all things start or end with an idea;
they happen like a montage in a film

for so long, then one day we wake to find
our thoughts are up and out before us,

out there on the road between the trees
at the edge of the lake – out there in the world –

the ceaseless flow beyond our windowpanes
that shapes us to its needs: the complex drift

of grasses in the rides, the river's spine,
the crimson thrill of dogwood in the snow,

the wildness that emerges at the edge
of what we know or what we think we know…

We only know these few things: this unplanned
appointment called a life; the earth inside

the marrow of our bones; this prize beyond
our habits and beliefs; the fading ink

in the footnotes to our deeds. For what
we seek in change is all the proof we need,

discovered where we least expect to find it,
as we continue on our journey to and from

being. We're only guests, just passing through
and always come back here before the end,

along the forest paths that bring us back
inside these bricks built round the central hearth;

this common space beyond our small conception
where we are called to things and rooted in

witness: the scent of dust on radiators,
woodworm leaving flight holes in the dresser,

a deathwatch beetle knocking in the beam –
the threads that knit uncertainties together,

making room for hope and trust and change;
these last stones in the walls of memory.

Becoming

In science class the children dip fine threads
in liquid-crystal jars : they watch their lives

emerge in patterned forms along each line,
then hang them to dry at the classroom's edge.

Happiness

for James Simpson

My father taught me how to catch a fish
and once I had that simple thing in hand
he showed me the pleasures of rising at dawn
to hide in the banks of the watercress stream
reeling in dace from the riffles and flats
in tune with the rhythms of solitude
and the rustling water rats deep in the rushes.

He showed me how to lose yourself in morning
with rod and reel and tackle; with hooks
and weights and inherited floats –
Coloured Wagglers, Sliders, Long Toms,
Trotters, Peacocks, Swingers, Pike Trolls,
Cork Bobs on reed stems, *Goose Quills* and *Chubbers.*

He taught me that at those hours you exist
in the Here & Now but, at the same time,
on every other river you have known –
the way one river summonses *all* rivers;
the way a bridge joins one bank to another –
with happiness's hooked fish in your bag.

A Lover's Discourse

for C.W.

i.
When the liquid mercury begins to shake
you can rest assured… here comes the earthquake.

ii.
For you I am the nascent drip
trembling at your grass blade's tip.

iii.
Lying in the grass, a glass between us,
we gazed up and traced the path of Venus.

iv.
As a grounds man venerates his lawn,
so you're my sward and sod from dusk 'til dawn.

v.
Whenever I am here I make the trek
that starts at your toes and ends around your neck.

vi.
I drive my fingers' Cadillac
across the desert of your back.

vii.
A trace of you remains when I'm alone,
like wax upon a lithographic stone.

viii.
Your letters are Rosetta Stones
for understanding you and your concerns.

ix.
Amazed that I found you, or you found me,
what surprises us more is we both, sometimes, agree.

x.
Love is only accurate up to a couple of hundred yards,
beyond that we need trust and faith and Valentine's cards.

xi.
As when a fire storm devastates the slope,
the man who has forgotten's stripped of hope.

xii.
You ask me if I think love ever can
last longer than a holiday suntan.

xiii.
I rubbed the suntan cream across your neck.
Later, I went diving on the wreck.

xiv.
A love poem is a station platform
as much as a sacred grove.

xv.
In accidents of sorts we soon discover
it's whom we *shouldn't* love that causes bother.

xvi.
The idea is old, the material new:
the *other*'s sure significant, but who?

Self Portrait at the Year's Turning

The morning light slips through the louvered slats.
You tug your mind from bed and start the day
with washing, toast and coffee, then switch on
much later with the radio, as though your life
were taking place elsewhere – the everyday
desire to see yourself as someone else:

the bright, imagined self behind your dreams;
the other you, the one that lives inside
the space between which one of you is 'you'
and those that are just possibilities. For when
it comes to being, don't we all do it
with *some* success, as we begin to learn
ourselves, balancing with grace like acrobats
turned out in the disguise each year creates?

Blackbird

Unwinding in a hammock, balanced, slung
between the apple tree and garden shed,
they swing where many others must have swung.

As the curved horizon turns wine-red
where only moments past it shone pale blue,
the shifting winds bring neither cloud

nor sunshine, but a blackbird's song –
a tune mislaid, but one they always knew
they knew. It keeps them hanging in its threads,

like children trembling on a ladder's rung:
the unknown in the gifts a blackbird brings,
the echoes of the songs it leaves unsung.

Suburban Plot

As we approach the garden plot,
there's something clearly wrong up there,
but *what*, exactly, isn't obvious:

the screws from the strap on the tool shed door
lie neatly laid in rows, upon the pile
of slabs we might, ourselves, one day position;

the door itself, improbably, off its hinges,
propped up against the ship-lapped side,
just as we prop ourselves when we take five.

It takes us five minutes to fathom out
what *has* happened here, what mystery unfolded...
but, yes, those jaded kids from the estate

have broken in, again, kicking their way
through barbed- and chicken-wire to scale the fence,
to scramble through brambles and run the risk

of landing face down in the nettle beds;
rooting through our gear to make a strange
creation of tools, up there beyond the path:

a scarecrow, built of rakes, Dutch hoes;
two trowels for hands in gardening gloves;
cloches draped across him like a toga,

before they doused him in the fuel they'd filched
from the neighbour's looted shed, committing him
to flames, as looks of violation licked

across his pumpkin face and he watched them
dance around, trashing stuff and asking
the shadowed and indifferent night
exactly why they shouldn't, what's at stake?

Cemetery Song

The hardest things to see are simply there:
the plot inside the yard that says *Reserved,*
a thrush's song arriving on the air

as sharp as a mason's chisel, somewhere
between these rows where strangers lie interred.
The hardest things to see are simply there:

your lover's face; the covered-up affair;
the running race and small child who came third.
Like thrush's songs arriving on the air

that take us by surprise, we're unprepared
for everyday events, they're too absurd.
The hardest things to see are simply there,

concealed by carelessness or *laissez-faire*
like bushes covering up a calling bird.
A thrush's song arriving on the air

connects us like an answer to a prayer
for problems we've denied, or just deferred.
The hardest things to see are simply there:
like thrushes' songs arriving on the air.

'The Rain Falls Gently on the Town'

after Arthur Rimbaud

The rain conjures things from *the almost* –
that precinct where the everyday occurs,
suddenly apparent and mysterious:

the scent of tar and concrete in your nose;
a builder's sandwich sodden on a wall;
the stripes of rainbows rising from a pond;
the distant squeaks of bike wheels, like birdcalls;

Children's mouths raised open to the skies;
streetlamps making evening's pavements gleam;
the church spire gazing down on lawns and drives
in a dream of the idea of home.

The rain conjures things from *the almost*:
the ball of experience left out in the yard;
the angel of an umbrella, abandoned on the road.

After Bottling

All I know of how to turn the harvest in this autumn
is little: stripping the canes of their berries,
snapping corn cobs from their stems
wrapped in the shrouds of their husks.

All I know of gleaning runner beans;
of cutting through the stems of broccoli,
or trimming the kale and stipes of chard
is little still but, thankfully, enough.

Of this, however, I am fairly sure:

we take the berries from the brier
and simmer our conserves; we twist
the pumpkins from their vines for pies
and lanterns for the porch at Hallowe'en;
we pluck the pears and float them in a syrup
like specimens in a specialist's jar;
we bottle the gages and simmer a sauce…
and in this preservation rests
the turning-in that everyone awaits,
which is all we can be sure of in this
temporary body we've borrowed from the ground.

Before then I hope I might make
some lasting jams, some sufficient preserves,
but don't suppose I'll put down in words
anything as perfect as the strawberry's heart,
the pink shank of rhubarb,
the crown globe of the artichoke.

All I can do is ready myself and start,
as when they opened the King and Queen's tomb
and found the honey still fresh in its jar
ten thousand years after bottling.

Picking Bullaces

for Matthew Francis

With sweet and bitter fused beneath a skin
that's black or white, they ululate their whereabouts
with sour calls and subtler clues, these bushes
blousy white like clerics' albs. They are
the Ace of Clubs of the hedgerows, the Cue Balls
of foragers, the Bull's-Eyes at the heart of our intent.
Bloomed in chalky blues, they used to stain
the shepherds' callused fingers, these wild *bullies*,
laced into the thorny brake at the edge of the lea.
We lean in and lunge for them like scuba divers
of the briars, sculling round their shoals like seal cubs
chasing prey. We cull their bulging yield,
laboriously, to lay them later on a slab of bread
with cheese and ale. Today, they're all that is the case.

Rewriting the Ground

for Kelvin Corcoran

We walk inside, among the trees, and taste
the scent of mulching leaf mould on the air.
We walk in on a track through shin-deep mud

like figures sinking in a birthday cake,
this locale of a myth called 'In-ger-land'.
Windblown rubbish clusters in the brier

where the motorway rewrites the meadow;
the meadow soon becoming little more
than a memory, like the signatures and names

of birds and plants now only found in books
as they are lost at last to common speech:
lady ferns, their fiddleheads unfolding;

the wet green mop of sundew and sphagnum;
a purposeful wren in the dense tissues
of the over storey filtering light;

a peregrine in stasis with the wind;
warblers in the canopy whose tongues
have kept a liquid diary of the day;

the spark of a kingfisher hunting for minnows
in the amber artery of the stream,
the world performing inches from its bill…

Surrounded by this constant hum of change,
our woodpecker eyes hammer into the world,
to witness it and stop it getting lost.

Selvage

> **Selvage**
> **1.** an edging that prevents cloth from unravelling.
> **2.** *Geol.* an alteration zone at the edge of a rock mass.
> **3.** the edge-plate of a lock with an opening for the bolt.

1.

The clothes you stitched were elegies to hope;
their sleeves like sails on vessels we could board
to leave for other lands, perhaps the ones
inhabited by those clever elves in books
who made new shoes for cobblers and their wives
and found their own needs satisfied when they
provided them with trousers, caps and shirts…

For that was when you most seemed *in yourself*,
sewing outfits we would wear to school,
adjusting clothes you'd picked up in the sales
to make them one size smaller, and so, fit.

When sewing, all else seemed to vanish,
like you'd been singing vespers and some part
of you we couldn't ever know was nourished…
like father, every evening, coming back
from digging out his day, up to his neck
in holes for road-pipes, terrified as he was
by confined spaces. He'd loose the back door's bolt
with its tell-tale squeak and dead-lock *thud*
and clack his pipe upon the table's edge,
setting simple choices out for us: 'Son,
dig deep enough straight down you'll come to China,'

then sitting to his beer, his meat and veg,
nodding in that tight-lipped way he had
'Inherited from all the men on his side
of the family.'
      But you…

2.

…You knew it all along the ways the self
avers its wits in everyday vignettes like these
and yet its dull insistence leaves us vague
impressions that its presence saves no more
than vulgar imitations of itself –
or *the idea of itself* – a common veil
with each edge stitched to stop it spooling off.

It locks in change, just as it oversees
the borderland between renewal and loss,
the boundaries we build and hide behind,
under the eaves of our habits and beliefs.

3.

But what is it, this vestige of a nerve
that keeps late vigil *out there* in the world –
not in the mind, nor in the muscled spine –
and salvages itself like flocks of geese
amassed on shelves of sand before they rise
into the air and head out on their voyage
to breeding grounds still packed in floes of ice –
easy over villages and vales
where children watch them hover past in V's;
out to sea where harbour seals dive deep
in search of shoals of herring, sild, sardines
and the magnetised muscles of elvers
easing themselves back into the estuary…

4.

I think of you darning on evenings
like these; on evenings when we sat alone
and you flicked your thimble over yards of cloth
and time lags
      like a needle
           picking-up stitches,
each memory a message neatly sewn
inside the neck to tell us who we are
and save us from the flight of our intentions:

the spring migration we have waited for,
the steep beginning of the selves we face.

Home / Leaving

Then one day it finally happens,
exhausted by routine and comfort
beneath which far stranger truths lie,
you walk to the avenue's end
keen to the fillip of birdsong
above the roaring soccer in the park.

Perhaps it is a summer's evening,
warm light on the copper beeches,
your neighbour sitting in her garden
watching it all go by – the cyclists
and joggers, the dutiful dog walkers,
the six year old boy and his friends
exercising their shooting genes;
those teenagers across the road, jumping
the picket fence, tramping the lawn.

You pass from cul-de-sac to cul-de-sac,
nothing moving, everything in place.
Even the wind avoids turning corners
upon the civil houses; their parked-up
four-by-fours; their brass knobs and bells.
You still have time to turn and run
the way you ran as a child, ringing
your neighbours' bells and disappearing
into bushes…
            You find the breach,
that alleyway from here to somewhere else
and happen on a table in a yard, where
a blackbird picks at the remnants of something,
the orange eclipse of its eye

drawing you into its skull and lifting you
up and away from the garden, beyond
the suburbs and their indecision,
flying over houses, pubs and churches,
winging over rail lines and stations,
following the courses of rivers and streams
in their restless drive to reach the sea
and a smudge of sky above a faint horizon.

2

*'He visto un arrabal infinito donde se cumple
una insaciada immortalidad de ponientes.'*

*'I have seen the city's infinite outskirts, which meet
the insatiable immortality of sunsets.'*

J.L. Borges

The Outskirts

i.m. Dereke Brown, after J. L. Borges

1. Rain

The evening slowly clarifies
as light rain now starts falling.
Falling, or fell, rain is a thing
that always happens in the *now*.

And yet whoever hears the rain
recalls a time when luck revealed
a rose we call 'felicité'
and the curious tinge of its blushes.

The rain that veils these windows
also brightens the autumn fruits
in gardens in forgotten suburbs
which now no longer exist. The moist

evening carries the voice of my father
coming home, strangely alive.

2. Angel

Where the sprawling districts overlap
I saw the painted houses; the houses decked
in daring colours. They were like flags –
blue flags as deep as the dawn.

Some were the colour of sunrise
and some still wore the tint of dawn.
With passion they outshone the angles
of murky and dejected corners.

I think of the man looking skyward
from his fervent courtyard;
of his sturdy arms and the grave bliss
in his vineyard eyes.

I push the gate and enter,
and he is waiting there,
and we both keep the secret, he and I,
as the pleasure of this moment soothes and passes.

3. *Sunset*

Sunsets are always upsetting,
both startling twilights
and the unadorned,
but most disturbing of all
is that desperate, final glow
that tinges the plains
when the horizon no longer recalls
the hubris of the Western sky.

It hurts to embrace that tense,
distinctive light,
which our fear of darkness
imposes on space
and which ceases
the way a dream is shattered
the moment we know
we are dreaming.

4. Twilight

An evening like Last Judgement –
beyond the Resurrection of the Dead.
Your street is an open wound in heaven.

I don't know if that lucency
burning in the depths
is your spirit or a sunset…

insistent, like a nightmare,
the unease weighs me down.
The fenced horizon grieves.

The world is useless, cast away.
In the sky it is still day, yet night lies
treacherous in the trenches.

Light now only lives in the rendered walls
and a hubbub of kids in the garden.
Is that a yew tree or devil peering over the gate?

So many countries all at once – field, suburbs, sky.
Today I was rich: streets, sunsets, the trance
of evening. Without them, I am nothing.

5. Ashes

The silent clash of sunsets
beyond the city's reaches;
the ever-falling rebels out of heaven;
treacherous white dawns that return again
and again from the vacant ends of time;
your verdant gardens in the rain;
the massive eyes on a child's toy purse
I was afraid to hold, or open,

and whose image comes back to me
night after night in dreams;
the change and echo we become;
the moon on the birch trees
like Elizabethan ladies painted white,
as calm as mothers;
shared nights, anticipated evenings;
poetry, whose sound is everything;
the ashes of my father
in the moist silence of the moor;
the Saxons, the Angles, the Danes
who never knew they fathered me.

Are these things also me,
or do they just unlock
the impossible formulas
of all that I shall never know?

6. Garden

The garden gate swings open
with the ease of a book
we have read many times

and, once inside,
we need never look
on what we know by heart.

We know the customs and the spirit
and the family sayings every clan
devises. There is no need to speak

or lie about privilege;
everything here knows us,
our failings and our fears.

This is the pinnacle;
what heaven may, perhaps, bestow:
not admiration and victory,

but simply being admitted
to everything that is,
as real as rocks, as trees.

7. *Music*

As tall as the evening,
he crosses the innocent garden
and is caught in the exact light
of the irreversible moment
that brings us *this* moon and *this* silence.

But he is also in an ancient
twilight at Stonehenge,
or descending the steps of a temple
that once was stone
but now is earthly dust;

or unlocking the perfect alphabet
encrypted in the other hemisphere's stars;
or scenting an English rose.
He is where the music plays,
in the mild blue of the sky,

in poetry and the solitude which seeks him.
He is in the fountain's mirror,
in the marble of time and the terrace
that looks out on this
his final sunset; his garden.

8. Shadows

The voice of the bird
disguised by twilight
is silent at last.
You wander the garden
wanting something, I know.

Another's sparkling flute,
the words of a poem
on someone else's lips,
the moonlight on the lane –
are these things, really, not enough?

Melancholy rain
falling on the patio…
sad you're not part of my days;
sad simply to reckon
syllables in the vacant night.

3

'I have always longed to be a part of the outward life, to be out there at the edge of things, to let the human taint wash away in emptiness and silence as the fox sloughs his smell into the cold unworldliness of water; to return to the town as a stranger.'

J.A. Baker, The Peregrine

Homing

Like that name on the tip of your tongue,
or the thing you now think you should know
but don't, somewhere else you also understand
you have to get back home to Ithaca; to Kansas.

Like the camel beneath the date palm,
the mammoth crossing the Bering Straits
and the rodent at the doorway to her hole,
the world is a home outside of yourself.

In that version of your life in which experience
hangs snagged like scraps of wool on wire fences;
in which you find yourself out on the road
no shoes on your feet and a smile on your face

walking into territories you never meant to go;
in that and every other version, *Home* was there
before you ever knew it, knew *of* it –
just as the future lived in you already.

When you have to head back from there,
head back walking; head back at the pace
of thought; set off before time catches up
with you deep in your deep nakedness.

Lambing at Gwernllertai

for Gordon Gwyllim

The ewes were lambing and the cows
housed in the barn against the snow.

When the cold snap finally started to swing
he'd drive out cartloads of their dung

and spread it widely on the fields,
to lie there on the surface of the world –

thin on the ridge and thick in the furrows,
ready for the plough. But for now

he laboured nights beneath the universe
on iced-up mountainsides, delivering

lambs from isolated ewes – the skins
of the dead on the backs of the orphans –

sleeping in the cab and surviving on tins
of fruit and the slow release of condensed milk.

The Woolbrook

for Jane Monson

And there we stood undressing where the shepherds used to flock to drench their stock and rinse their fleeces in the ford. There, where the river slices through the hazel break and the world meanders on in all its detail: mayfly larvae underneath the stones; magnified minnows beneath the water's lens; caddis flies inside their jewelled sleeves; dace and roach in the channels and troughs where they first began as fingerlings, immersed in the flow, in the real.

We doused our summer heads in the freezing stream and threw off our shirts to lunge in naked, joined to the stalk of friendship like the trefoil of a clover, enjoying the quick run of golden water between the granite boulders, between our shoulder blades and down our backs (were they aching or arching?) before we dressed and ran on ourselves to the clapper bridge to race sticks underneath its granite arches.

No single drop escapes they say. Even the seas that Moses parted, the lake the Buddha's lotus sprang from, still exist somewhere… molecules, packed in polar ice-caps, waiting…

Pen y Fan

We have been climbing since well before dawn
and now we're alone: the *couloir* unclouded,
no skirl of wind, and all around a budding
riotousness.   Astray in the mountainous heart.

We make the peak and try to fit a landscape
into notebooks. Things emerge out of the blue:
loose ribbons of side-tracks; the glint of gneiss;
a beehive cairn at the precipice edge.

Can anything answer the reason we're here;
the things outside that silhouette the inner?
A cricket chirrs, a raven krekks

caught in the shadow of a simple thought –
wherever we go we are guests to the world
like tufts of sheep's wool snagged on stands of whin.

How to Pay Attention

Just over there stand the herons
essential and still on the groynes:
spying out prey in the shallows,
cracking crabs with sinuous jabs
and spearing rock pool minnows.

The herons have no name
for the shellfish and fingerlings
they catch in the weedy lagoon;
they patiently stand there and watch
the calm at the end of their bills.

The herons possess their own quarter
completely, until we arrive
to name them – 'crab' and 'heron' –
shattering their given moment
like a stone dropped through sheet-ice…

Then they're in takeoff, the herons:
a loping procession above the trees
towards invisibility, across the sound,
leaving us to our conversation
and the pull of the turning tide.

The Wood for the Trees

Just as what we recognize as *us*
lies outside as much as within,
so those cushions of leaf fall
and humus pile up on the ground

in the forests we've led ourselves into,
where woodpigeons *troo-loo*
and animals and men act out
their uncertain roles.   The trees

don't recognize us in any of this:
their polyglot melange of leaves
describes the light effortlessly.
They have such beautiful handwriting

the trees. They make their own place
in all this unruliness, forever emerging.
Do we see the trees – *the things
themselves* – or just a doubtful haze?

The birch trees bend; the wood unlocks.
What we know is a step towards
the prospect of change; putting faith
in the world's offertory box.

Crow Wedding

> 'We asked for wings that we might test the sky;
> you gave us earth that we might test our wings.'
> *Prayer*

I want to give thanks for this meadow
in the middle of nowhere-but-here,
wrapped up in the hum of events;

for its rings of toadstools
in the fog of its grass;
for its opus of Friesians
by the woodwind copse;

for the quarrelsome wren
burrowed deep in the bush
and the birdcall that turns us
on our stretch of dirt road;

for the whirr of the dragonfly
on its thistle-head perch
and the badger cubs trowelling
the friable earth
where the metropolitan ant
and the ordered bee
have made
their impermanent homes;

for the caterpillar slung
from a gossamer thread
and the clear blades of light
through the canopy leaves
that somehow slice it free…

I want to give thanks
for the wedding of crows —
two high birds diving
down and down,
upon their dropped
upon their tumbling
stone.

On Coupling

The wheatear scrapes her scruffy little cup
by the dry stone wall; the lark spirals up.

The finch explores between stonecrop and gorse
seeking a mate, and the harrier, of course

cares for none of this – she flags her white rump,
flexes her wings on the boundary stump

and starts her laboured, ruthless flight,
combing the bedstraw's purple froth for mice.

Two Birdstrikes

1.

We clatter through horsetails
dwarf birch trees and sedge
and startle a buzzard
with our twig-snapping boots.

She sparks from the phone wire
and stooks hard away,
her quick green eyes flushing
her kill from the lee.

The evergreen moss.
A rabbit's warm entrails.
This world and its manifest things.

2.

As evening claims our minds
so waders claim the lake,
stilting the shin-high fertile muck,
the layered museum of the tarn.

A heron poles away from shore
as, down, with sharp baptismal cries
the falcon falls to snatch a silvered
muscle through the sundered blue.

Nocturne

Beyond the ruins of the timber yard
where clumps of rowan, birch and alder
stand ringed with wire against the hungry deer,
the earth is wrought by badger runs.

The dusk is animals – the shrieks of vixens,
owls and fleeting bats – and, if you press
your ear against the evening's broad door
you may hear them: the mother badger,

her heavy skull, her jaws, her glinting teeth
and these, her badger cubs – their mellow baying;
their barrel bodies crashing through the tumps,
writing what they mean in flattened grass.

They grope for teats along her yielding belly,
taking the night on their own terms:
theirs is the world that persists in our absence.
We emerge from the dark with our lamps,

through the gaps in the trees where the copse
meets the meadow and leave them to reclaim
their glade, as dawn grows imperceptibly from night
and presses upwards with the thought of dew.

Forest

> It is common knowledge that the forest
> echoes back what you shout into it.
> *Karl Marx*

Forest seems to rest in silence,
but while the wood has ears and listens
forest really resonates with tongues.
Forest rings with old intensities.
Forest is the greatest filter.
Forest is the store of rain,
is strangely renewed by fire.
Dense, impenetrable, forest starts
where forest is imagined. Forest is
the warehouse of the word of the world.
Weird forest, written forest;
forest of tomorrow's news,
where forests of ideas become
a busy public library. Medicinal
forest where forest is the cure.
Forest is as forest won't forget.
Forest that once led us to the point
of being lost. Forest that named us
and showed us the whole to be
the sum of forest. Forest that fastens
shore to far-off shore. Endless forest
of fable and tale, the Brothers Grimm,
the forest Borges dreamed. Forest
that centres the universe, that tests
the idea of the tree that falls
when no one's there to hear it.

Forest that once was our walking
and our waking. The ever growing
forest in the wind like groaning stanchions.
Forest that dropped the growth
that was the making of itself.
Forest the eye can readily reach,
that eyes cannot traverse. Charmed,
unruly forest of the seen and the unseeable.

But forest is a memory. Forest slashed
and forest burned. Forest is denuded ground,
is cleared, stands stripped by sour rains.
Forest, overgrown and undermanaged.

From pollen study to pathology,
forest holds the secrets of our myths
and of our laxity. Forest is remembrance
of the hunt in the forest. It hunkers there
and howls, like an angry wolf.

Learning the Names

> 'Learning the names is a method of noticing.'
> William Fiennes, *The Snow Geese*

The season's just beginning. Under birch and alder
the breath of sleeping roe deer fills the hollows.
Last night's badgers have tattered a hole
in the mineral soil: the thicket's floor
stippled with king ferns, their crosiers curled
like babies' fists;   a history in bud.
We used to know the world by name,
but what does it matter, the flower's name,
if we can't recall its smell, or where to find it?
A pair of buzzards wing their ragged way
through tiers of poplars clacking in the wind,
naming things with nothing more than vision;
their cries sending hares over aits and streams,
their hooked bills keen to scent the coming rain.

Harbour Blues

The blue hills to the estuary's far shore
cast shadows on the tall ships in the bay,
vast presences beneath their ordered rigs:

the sailing boats return with tired crews;
the blue sky darkens as the dark shore blues.

The anchored yachts shift, pitching on the swell.
Seaplanes and taxi boats putter down the lanes
in a slow procession beyond the harbour wall:

the dolphin boats return with elated crews;
the blue sky darkens as the dark shore blues.

The mackerel shoals are running past the point
following the sprats. My thoughts are out at sea
reeling in ravenous muscles of light:

the fishermen return with fanciful news;
the blue sky darkens as the dark shore blues.

In the cradled horseshoe of the bay, the kids
hunt peeler crabs reclusive under rocks;
build driftwood huts beyond the water mark:

they wander home, replete, with salt-caked shoes;
the blue sky darkens and the dark shore blues.

The Storm Berm

Our dinghy wallows and the water swears
to pitch us into the elating world
of dogfish and bass, where the earth falls off;
where thunder rolls in with a probing light.

Behind us, doe-eyed harbour seals disturb
the surface, their knowing bodies rolling
underneath, stirring strong eddies and whorls.

Ahead the water bends into the creek
between the buoys that mark the shallow strait.
Our boat restores its pitch and makes the quay
busy now with labouring fishermen

piling sandbags high onto the berm.
We moor and join them, shoring our defence
against the rising tide; the coming storm.

A Beach

for Lee Harwood

From an infinite mixture of sand grains,
across vast spans of time, laid down
by violent waves and rock erosion,
the uniform shoreline emerges.
Despite the constant changes of the tides;
despite the constant shifting of the sands,
there it is today, and then again today.

I wake from my dream of the beach –
the scald of hot sand on my soles;
crystal castles in a summer parade;
shifting forms beneath the fish-scale sea.
Like the beach, I wake and make myself
anew: the cells of my body today
are not those 'I' was born with;
the hormones of my body as I wake,
different from those in my bloodstream
last night. I feel a self, but can't locate it…

The ever changing beach begins its day
the same way that a seed constructs
a flower; the nut a tree; the ant or bee
her colony; the starling her flock;
like a city built from bottom up;
the cell, the human body; the endless shifting sea.

Seascape with Kites and Gulls

> ...the love that consists in this: that two solitudes
> protect and border and greet each other.
> Rilke, Letter 7,
> *Letters to a Young Poet*

Summer called them from the port of desire,
with its loud, insistent reach towards the future;
those fields of days that stretch and yearn
beyond the compass span of 'yes' or 'no'.
That morning on the bight they stood and watched
the coastal sky sparkling with kites –
*Twisters, Quadlines, Chevrons, Trackers,
Speedwings, Prisms, Spinoffs, Fighters* –
their pilots keen to keep firm hold,
but oh how they wanted to let go.
They watched each flyer test the sky
and wondered how their blend of luck and skill
kept some up in the blue, while others hovered
just above the sand in perfect stasis,
or crashed in nosedives, broken on the rocks.
Certainly the gulls knew how *they* felt –
hungry, territorial – tossing out waste from the bins,
exploring it with forceful, stabbing bills;
spreading their wings in expansive displays
to frighten off a rival, stake their claim.
In that moment, they felt they saw themselves:
the brilliant light with its scarf of clouds;
the kites;
   the gulls;
      the patient vocabulary of trust.

Song of the Lifeboat Men's Daughters

>   'My ghostly constant is articulated.'
>   W.S. Graham, 'The Nightfishing'

They tack along the shipping lanes in search
of the lost. Through the pilothouse window
the landmasses dwindle to pinpoints; lines
of lanterns swinging from pilings and piers.

Nearing the strait where most boats turn turtle,
the greatest risk lies not somewhere beneath,
but closer to the surface, shadowed by
the fear that bonds with silence to produce
rocky shores and reefs as if from nowhere.

Endlessly wind-blown, the storm petrels drop –
dark silhouettes of the living. Our fathers
watch anchor buoys in lines across the spines
of wave crests; an armada of seagulls
resolving cliffs by soaring. They roll in
the night gales; hang motionless mid-breaker;
listen to the yowls of the black-backed gulls –
those avatars of the very darkness – sitting on
the anchor's prongs.
        But soon the captain's smile
will climb to daybreak, and our dreams? Our dreams
become a crew of sea-sprayed men returning home,
hauling their heavy vessel up the shingle.

Scraping salt from our faces, we do not know
if we have been crying or out at sea ourselves.

A Ship in a Bottle

Inside the bottle, a ship. How it came to be there, we may never know exactly – some trick with a knife and a drawstring – but the ship *is there*, inside the bottle. A ship with high-curving bows and dawn light flecking her rigging.

Inside the rigging, little sound or movement. But press your ears against the planks and you will hear the echo of hammers and saws; the footsteps of a sailor stealing a sunbeam or two at the prow, as his mates haul their nets, watching the sky for changes.

In the sky around the masts, seabirds fly – soaring, stalling, plunging to the wake. They hang and turn, fly upside down and cry, landing on the ropes and beams to gain respite, then, garrulous into the air: windblown harpies with their ever-present hunger.

The sea too is hungry. Feeders everywhere have made their kill – diving gannets, rising sei whales, leopard seals and blue sharks through the shoals. It is a harmful sea, yet inside a crescent of nursing whales, their young protected from attack. On board, inside the galley, the cook blends up a breakfast of soup and pickled herring.

Inside his mess, the captain sleeps through dawn. Throughout the night the seas of his dreams have blundered against his ship, drawn over waves by the wink of a lighthouse that picks out blunt shoulders of rock. Above his crow's nest, thunderheads form cliffs. Inside his dreams the ocean beats all night, sloshing holes in shelves of rock he navigates with ease.

Ashore, inside the harbour with its horseshoe line that everybody trusts, the old retired vessels rest and list on a scallop of sand. Beneath the wall a pile of nets, of creels and buoys, piled up there by the fisherman who ties his dinghy to the pier before returning home to spend his evening putting ships in bottles.

Inside each bottle he hangs the sunlit rim of the sea, curving from the distant whine and crash of breakers to headlands of quiet anchorage topped by a sailors' chapel. Inside each chapel, a team of sailors praying. Above the gravestones in the quiet yard, prayer birds stir their wing tips in an act of ocean wondering. Inside the graves of the drowned, the prehistoric sea rinses the bones.

Along the Tide Wash

for Richard Beard

Coursing the great jugulars of rivers,
our little boats now try to ply the routes,
keening where the seasons take them.
Our elders' journeys followed other streams.

Our little boats now try to ply the routes.
The water shines in memory of the sky.
Our elders' journeys followed other streams.
To throw off our clothes and plunge in naked!

The water shines in memory of the sky,
an endless strand emerging from the tide.
To throw off our clothes and plunge in naked;
to dash in the surf in defiance of death…

An endless strand emerges from the tide –
the bluff of land at the estuary's mouth.
To dash in the surf in defiance of death…
Out on the mud flats, change lies anchored.

The bluff of land at the estuary's mouth –
hooked like the kype of a migrating salmon.
Out on the mud flats, change lies anchored,
aching for the land like a sluggish river.

Hooked like the kype of a migrating salmon,
the ribcage of a wreck buried in black silt.
It aches for the land like a sluggish river,
this equinoctial haze; this white weather.

The ribcage of a wreck buried in black silt;
avocets and cormorants rising off the water;
this equinoctial haze; this white weather;
these are facts here, snared in trolling lines.

Avocets and cormorants rise off the water.
Distant figures hasten through the wetness.
These are facts here, snared in trolling lines,
driven by what little we encounter.

Distant figures hasten through the wetness,
keening where the seasons take them,
driven by what little they encounter,
coursing the great jugulars of rivers.

It Happens When You Look Away

'The first thing you'll see is the blow,'
the whale guide said, 'that tall spume
of air and mist the animals release
as they come to the surface to breathe.'

You waited; the sheer world honing:
the sky blue mirror of the ocean, rill'd
with the comings-and-goings of fish
and diving birds unmindful of your presence.

The up-and-down shifts in the bones of your ears
stayed keen to the tiniest change in the wind
as if it might signal the probable spray…

and still you gazed, unsure, into the gulf
at gulls, a seal, the light that conjures shapes
that vanish, suddenly, into the blue.

Matriline

Across the *Juan De Fuca Straits*
shoals of clouds – grey, black and white –
muscle in between two worlds. Terns
stitch the frills, quicker than boats,

their bright cries merging with other-
worldly sounds – clicks, chirrups, coos –
a mother and her newborn calf
breaching beneath the mind's hull.

Planktos

planktos: 'wandering' or 'drifting'

Evening finds us in the resting place
of a sailboat smashed on rocks.

A cascade burls a cleft into the cliff
where martins flit to feed their young.

Tonight is fit a night as any for a fire –
the driftwood of the changes never made.

Secure in the circle of our desires, we
burn candour far into the night. The sea

goes mad within the limits of the sea.
We pull ourselves in on ropes of memory.

The Last Geese

Partway there the tarmac vanishes, doubling back
in a blend of bayberry and heath; fringed dunes
where sparse grass forms a false horizon
between the pond-pocked leas. You have to proceed
from here on foot, parking by the haunting shapes
of padlocked beach huts skulking by the harbour.
Above, on phone wires, starlings string like beads,
while down below a fisherman trawls a line
clutching at the magnetised muscles of fish –
single mullet, flounder, bass – flipping them
finally into his bucket before he hacks off a head,
tossing the guts to a rabble of gulls on the wind.

Then a new sound – geese the size of the wind
taxiing over the crests and lifting their heads
above the port wall, a whistling tail wind pushing them
into the open bay, over the empty depths of fish,
the fishermen's buoys laid out in hopeful lines
marking crab and lobster creels like precious beads.
Their wings shadow the cradle of the harbour
as they follow the spring migration north, their shapes
lacing the downward shafts of light as they proceed
through the pink keyhole of the horizon.
You launch a shrill honk onto the air from the dunes.
The parting geese reply; the unseen echoing back.